W9-CNF-578

DISCARD

ALL ABOUT WHALES
Dorothy Hinshaw Patent

© PETER THOMAS

J
599.51
P

88/4

Holiday House/New York

51236

For kids who love whales
D. H. P.

Thanks to Peigin Barrett of the
California Marine Mammal Center
for her time and interest.

Copyright © 1987 by Dorothy Hinshaw Patent
All rights reserved
Printed in the United States of America
First Edition

Library of Congress Cataloging-in-Publication Data

Patent, Dorothy Hinshaw.
All about whales.

Includes index.
SUMMARY: An introduction to the biggest animal that
ever lived, discussing what it eats, how it communicates,
and the kinds of whales.
1. Whales—Juvenile literature. [1. Whales] I. Title.
QL737.C4P3738 1987   599.5   86-27126
ISBN 0-8234-0644-X

Contents

This 60-foot-long blue whale was stranded on a beach in California. ALISA SCHULMAN

I

What Are Whales?

Whales are the biggest animals that ever lived. The largest kind, the blue whale, is as long as seven or eight cars lined up end to end. Even the smallest whales are bigger than people. All whales live in the sea, but they are not fish. They are mammals, like dogs and horses.

*The humpback whale has a
two-part blowhole.*
J. MICHAEL WILLIAMSON

Whales as Mammals

All animals need oxygen to survive. Fish get oxygen from the
water, but mammals get it from breathing air. The whale has a
special hole on the top of its head for breathing. It is called the
blowhole. When a whale comes to the surface of the water, it lets
old air out through the blowhole. This makes a spout called the
blow. When the whale breathes, it brings fresh air into the blowhole. The whale holds its breath when it dives. The blowhole
closes over when the whale is underwater.

The blow of a blue whale. NOAA

Most mammals have hair. But the only hairs on a whale are a few stiff bristles on its snout. Some whales don't even have these. Hair can slow down a swimming animal. Over time, whales have lost their hair. Their skin is smooth and rubbery, which makes swimming easier.

If you look closely where the arrow is pointing, you can see bristles on the head of this gray whale.
C. ALLAN MORGAN

Unlike fish, mammals have warm bodies, even in cold water. A mammal's hair helps keep it warm. Instead of hair, whales have a thick layer of fat under their skin, called blubber. The blubber protects them from cold water. A blue whale's blubber can be a foot (30.5 centimeters) thick. The whale's large size also helps it keep warm. A big animal loses heat more slowly than a small one.

Other Whale Traits

Whales are different from fish in other ways, too. A fish has a tail that moves back and forth when it swims. There are bones in a fish's tail. A whale has a big tail with two halves called flukes. But the flukes have no bones. They are made of tough fibers. Whales have long muscles in their bodies that are attached to the fibers and pull the flukes up and down as the whale swims.

The flukes of a humpback whale. DAVIES/GREENPEACE

A whale has a pair of flippers on its sides which have bones in them like our arms do. The flippers help the animal steer as it swims.

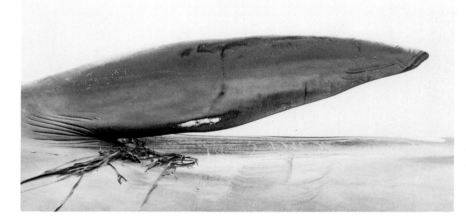

A flipper of a fin whale.
NOAA

In this skeleton of a killer whale, you can see the bones of the flipper spread out at the lower right. Although the flipper does not have fingers, the finger bones are there.
S. HEIMLICH / GREENPEACE

*The humpback has a
small dorsal fin.*
STEPHEN MULLANE

Most whales also have a dorsal fin on the back. It helps keep the
body stable during swimming.

*The killer whale has a
very tall dorsal fin.*
© PETER THOMAS

There are many kinds of whales. Some whales have teeth and are closely related to dolphins and porpoises. Other whales have no teeth at all. Instead they have baleen (bay-LEEN). Baleen is made up of plates of material, like huge, thick, flat fingernails, that hang down from the upper jaws. Whales use the baleen to strain food from the water.

The pilot whale has sharp teeth.
VINCENT SERVENTY

The baleen of the gray whale.
© *ALLAN MORGAN*

2
Whales with Teeth

Killer whales and sperm whales have teeth. So do the less familiar belugas (be-LOU-gas), narwhals (NAR-wahls), and beaked whales. Most of these whales feed on fish and squid. They have a fatty bump on the head called the melon. They also have a single blowhole.

Killer whales have strong, pointed teeth. The bump on the forehead is called the melon. DOTTE LARSEN

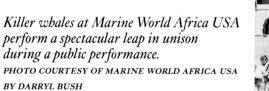

Killer whales at Marine World Africa USA perform a spectacular leap in unison during a public performance.
PHOTO COURTESY OF MARINE WORLD AFRICA USA
BY DARRYL BUSH

The Killer Whale

Killer whales are familiar to many people. They perform at marine parks like Marine World Africa U.S.A. Killer whales have striking black and white patterns, and they live in groups called pods. A pod may have up to fifty members. They eat fish, seals, penguins, and sea turtles.

Killer whales are not as big as some other kinds. A male may be more than 30 feet (9 meters) long. Females are usually shorter than 21 feet (6.4 meters). These animals live in oceans around the world.

The Sperm Whale

The sperm whale is a strange looking animal. It has a huge square head with a narrow bottom jaw. The blowhole is way out on the left side of the tip of its "nose." Inside the head is a sac containing a fine oil called spermaceti (sper-mah-SET-ee). Under the sac is an area of spongy cells containing a different kind of oil. Thousands of sperm whales were killed during the eighteenth and nineteenth centuries for the oil in their heads.

A sperm whale.
VINCENT SERVENTY

13

The sperm whale is very big. Males are sometimes 60 feet (18.3 meters) long. Females may be as long as 40 feet (12.2 meters). These giants dive to at least 4,000 feet (1,220 meters), where they feed on squid. They can stay underwater for more than an hour.

Sperm whales also live in pods, especially the females and young. Females stay in warm tropical waters, but full-grown males travel thousands of miles. They feed in northern and southern seas most of the year. They only return to the tropics to mate.

A sperm whale blows between deep dives. Noitce the small dorsal fin and the blowhole, which is out on the left side of the tip of the "nose." GEORGE VAN DOREN

A *beluga.* ALISA SCHULMAN

Arctic Whales

The beluga and the narwhal are small whales that live in the north. Both lack a dorsal fin and have thick skin and a very thick blubber layer. This helps protect them from the cold Arctic climate.

The beluga is light brown or pinkish gray when young, and white when grown up. It lives in the open water during the winter and moves into the mouth of a river for the summer. Belugas often travel in huge pods. More than 10,000 may be together at one time. In Russian waters, belugas may reach 21 feet (almost 7 meters) in length. In other areas, they are smaller, sometimes no bigger than 13 feet (4 meters).

Narwhals are about the same size as belugas. They also travel in pods. The narwhal is unique among whales. The front tooth on the left side of males grows through the upper lip and sticks straight out in front. It may be as long as 10 feet (3 meters). The purpose of this tusk is a mystery. Male narwhals have been seen crossing tusks, possibly in battle. But some scientists think the tusk is used to carry sounds for communicating with other narwhals.

Narwhals live along the edge of the sea ice. They are still hunted by natives for their tusks, meat, blubber, and skin.

In this skull, you can see clearly that the narwhal tusk comes from the left side of the head. (Photo taken at the Los Angeles Museum of Natural History.) ALISA SCHULMAN

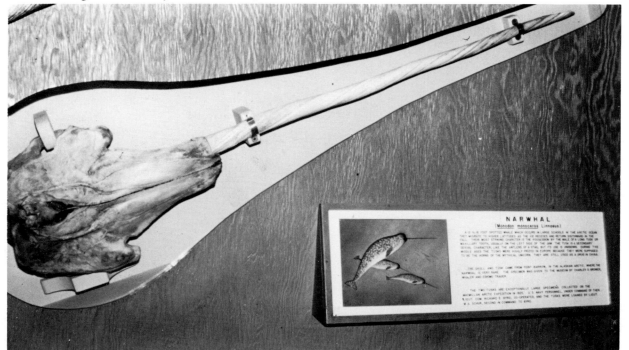

Other Toothed Whales

There are many less familiar kinds of toothed whales. The dwarf and pygmy sperm whales look like their large cousin, the sperm whale. Pilot whales live in big pods, as does the false killer whale. There is also a pygmy killer whale, which reaches a length of only 8 feet (2.4 meters) as well as small melon-headed whales.

Beaked whales are very large and live in the ocean depths. Little is known about them, although there are eighteen different kinds. No one even knows if these mysterious animals are rare or if they just stay far from shore.

The short-finned pilot whale is a small whale. Males get to be 19.5 feet (5.9 meters) long, but females reach only about 13 feet (4 meters) in length. © ALLAN MORGAN

3
Baleen Whales

Baleen whales are the biggest animals of all. A female blue whale can reach 100 feet (30 meters) in length and weigh 150 tons (136 metric tons). Even the biggest dinosaurs were not that large. Besides the sperm whale, the baleen whales were the ones most prized by whalers, for their meat, blubber, and baleen. Several kinds almost became extinct from hunting. Now their numbers are partly protected by international agreement.

Baleen whales have a two-part blowhole. A ridge reaches from the tip of the snout to the blowhole. The sides of the ridge spread around the blowhole so that it sticks up a little above the top of the head.

Baleen whales, like this humpback, are big animals. You can see here that the whale's fin is about as big as the whale watchers on the boat. © BRUCE M. WELLMAN

The upper jaw of a fin whale, showing the baleen on both sides of the mouth.
KEN BALCOMB/ORES

The plates of baleen hang down around the edges of the mouth from the top jaw. Each plate is about one-fourth inch (0.63 centimeters) thick. The plates are usually around one-fourth inch apart. Each plate is shaped like a triangle. The inside edges of the baleen are frayed.

The baleen rims both sides of the mouth. There can be 450 plates on each side of the jaw. The plates can also be very big. Blue whales have wide, short baleen. It is almost 2 1/2 feet (76 centimeters) wide, but it is no longer than 2 feet (60 centimeters). Right whales have long, narrow baleen. It is less than a foot (30.5 centimeters) wide, but it may be 7 feet (about 2 meters) long.

Baleen whales feed on fish and very small animals that live in the water. They take food-laden water into their mouths. Then they let the water out through the gaps between the baleen plates. The food is held in the mouth by the frayed inner edges of the baleen.

Streamlined Whales

The blue, fin, sei (say), Bryde's (BRU-duhz), and minke (MINK-ee) whales are all designed for fast swimming. They have slim bodies with a dorsal fin set far back on the body. They are some of the fastest swimmers in the sea.

These whales are called rorquals (ROAR-kwelz). This name comes from the Norwegian word for furrow. A rorqual has long grooves on the underside of its body. The grooves allow the throat to expand while the whale is feeding.

This close-up photo shows the grooves on the throat of a humpback whale.
ALISA SCHULMAN

The minke whale is the smallest rorqual at 33 feet (10 meters) long. There are actually three types of minke whale. Northern minke whales have a white band on each flipper, while the southern ones lack this marking. A third type was recently discovered off the coast of Brazil. It is smaller than the other two and has different markings.

The sei and Bryde's whales are medium-sized and are about 65 feet long (19.8 meters). Bryde's whale lives in the tropics, while sei whales migrate, following the fish they eat.

This young minke whale was stranded on a beach and died. Notice that the baleen isn't fully grown yet. ALISA SCHULMAN

The back of a sei whale. Notice the strange scars, which may be caused by a parasite or a cookie-cutter shark. ALISA SCHULMAN

A fin whale at the water's surface. You can see the mist left over from its blow above the blowhole. STEPHEN MULLANE

Fin whales can reach 88 feet (27 meters) in length. They have a white patch on the right side of the face. The baleen on the right side is also white. Scientists think this strange color pattern might be involved in feeding.

The enormous blue whale is hard to imagine. It can weigh as much as thirty-three elephants. Its heart is as big as a small car. Its stomach can hold two tons (1.8 metric tons) of food. Even so, it is a graceful animal. It can swim as fast as 30 miles (48 kilometers) per hour and can turn quickly.

This blue whale has just let out air from its enormous blowhole. GREENPEACE

The Humpback

The humpback doesn't look like other rorquals, but scientists put it in the same family because of its grooved throat. The humpback is plump, and it has the longest flippers of all the whales. They are about one-third the length of the body. The humpback has knobs with bristles on its head.

More is known about humpbacks than most other whales. They are found in many seas and migrate along both the eastern and western coasts of America. Humpbacks are famous for their unique songs and for the many ways they catch food.

This humpback whale is breaching—throwing itself up out of the water. When it lands, it makes a very big splash that can sometimes be heard for miles. STEPHEN MULLANE

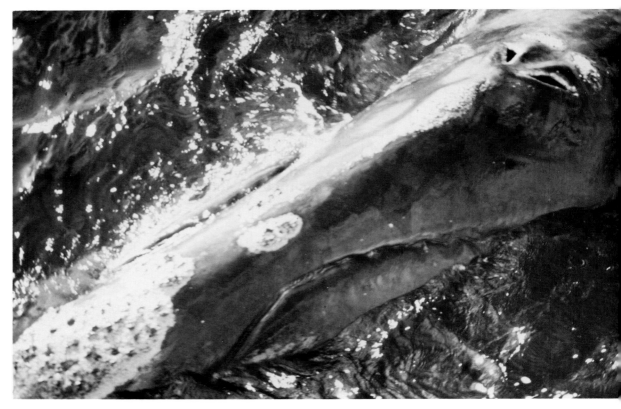

*You can see the callosities on the top
of the head of this right whale.
The blowhole is at the upper right, and the
curved edges where the upper and lower
jaws meet can also be seen.*
ANN G. RIVERS

The Right Whales

The black right whale was once the most common kind in the North Atlantic Ocean. Now, because of whaling, it is very rare. This stocky animal was considered the "right" whale to kill. It swam slowly, had lots of useful baleen and blubber, and floated when dead.

The black right whale has a curved mouth covering its long flexible baleen plates. It has strange bumps on its head called callosities (kal-OS-it-eez). Since each animal has a different pattern of callosities, researchers are able to identify individual whales.

The Greenland right whale is more often called the bowhead. Its mouth is even more curved than the black right whale's. Like the black right whale, it has no dorsal fin. The bowhead lives in the Arctic. It, too, was a favorite with whalers. Now it is closer to extinction than any other big whale.

The pygmy right whale is the smallest great whale. It is only about 20 feet (6.1 meters) long and is slimmer than other right whales. It has a small dorsal fin.

The Gray Whale

Gray whales once lived in both the North Atlantic and the North Pacific oceans. Now, because of whaling, they are only found in the Pacific. They migrate about 10,000 miles (16,100 kilometers) each year along the western coast of America. They feed in Arctic seas during the summer and give birth in the winter in Mexican waters. The gray whale stays in shallow water along the coasts.

Sometimes, whales get stranded in shallow water, like this young gray whale. The people are splashing water on its back to keep it from drying out. © PETER THOMAS

4
How Whales Grow

Here is a mother sei whale with her calf. ALISA SCHULMAN

We know little about how whales mate because they are so hard to watch. Like almost all other mammals, whales give birth to live young. Whales usually have only one baby at a time, and twins are very rare. A baleen calf is born ten to twelve months after mating. Toothed whales carry their young for over a year.

The Newborn Whale

Newborn whales can be very large. A sperm whale calf is 12 to 14 feet (3.7 to 4.3 meters) long at birth and weighs about a ton (900 kilograms). A baby blue whale starts out at 7.5 tons (6.8 metric tons) in weight and 20 to 25 feet (6.1 to 7.6 meters) in length.

This baby killer whale looks small compared to its mother, but it was already 8 feet (2.4 meters) long when it was born.
CHIP MATHESON

The mother whale takes good care of her baby. When it is born, she helps it up to the surface to get its first breath of air. Her nipples are hidden in two grooves on her belly. When the calf is hungry, it nudges the mother. Her nipples then stick out from the groove. The baby takes a nipple deep inside its mouth. Then the mother squirts milk out rapidly. The baby can only nurse for a few seconds at a time since it must surface often for air. But in that time, gallons of milk go down its throat.

Whales have very rich milk. It is as much as 50 percent fat. Cow's milk is only about 4 percent fat. Not only is the milk rich, but there is plenty of it. A large mother whale produces more than 130 gallons (492 liters) of milk for her baby each day.

This gray whale traveled to the warm, shallow waters of San Ignacio Lagoon in Mexico to have her calf.
ALISA SCHULMAN

Growing Up

Most whales migrate to warm waters when the young are born. This helps protect the babies, since they have only a thin layer of blubber at first.

Baby whales grow fast on their rich milk diet. The blue whale is the fastest-growing animal on earth. It gains an average of almost 8 1/2 pounds (3.9 kilograms) an hour from the time it is born until it is seven months old.

Young whales nurse from their mothers for a year or two. Then they can feed on their own. Humpbacks have a calf every two or three years. Some killer whales, however, may reproduce only once in seven years.

The Family Group

Some whales are very social animals. Killer whale pods seem to be family groups. The young stay in the same pod with the mother even after they are grown up. New animals probably join the pod only through birth and seem to leave only when they die.

Some scientists think that whales help one another in caring for the young. Sperm whales dive very deep to feed. The young whale can't go along with its mother. Scientists have seen one adult sperm whale at the surface with two calves. They think the adult was "baby-sitting" for a mother that had gone to feed. They also saw a sperm whale being born. Very quickly, several whales came over to the baby. They nudged it and rubbed up against it. They even lifted it out of the water. They seemed to want to get as close to the new whale as possible.

A pod of killer whales. You can see both adults and young whales in this picture. GREENPEACE

5
How Whales Eat

It takes a lot to feed a whale. A blue whale can eat as much as 4 tons (3.6 metric tons) each day! Even the much smaller killer whale needs plenty of food. Killers at Sea World can put away 125 pounds (57 kilograms) of fish in a day. Whales have several different ways of feeding.

While killer whales eat lots of fish, they also attack seals and, as in this photo, sea lions. JEFF FOOTT/DRK PHOTO

Killers in a Pack

Killer whales are sometimes called "the wolves of the sea." This is a good name for them because they often hunt in a pack. By joining together, the whales can successfully attack big animals like seals. One scientist watched a pod of killer whales hunt a seal that was resting on a small iceberg. Several whales swam together toward the iceberg. They used their flukes to make a big wave that tipped the iceberg over, dumping the seal into the water. Killers may even attack blue whales.

Killer whales also feed on fish and often follow migrating salmon.

Killer whales feeding together. CHIP MATHESON

The Sperm Whale Mystery

Because sperm whales dive so deep, no one can see just how they feed. But scientists can look into the stomachs of dead whales to see what they have eaten. Sperm whales feed mostly on squid of all sizes. They can even attack giant squid that may be 60 feet (18.3 meters) long.

The sperm whale's mouth is small for its size, and most of the squid in its stomach is whole. Scientists watching these animals believe that the teeth are not important in feeding. The teeth in the lower jaw are big, but there are no teeth to be seen in the upper jaw. Healthy whales with twisted jaws that couldn't be used properly have been found. So how do they catch their food?

One whale expert, Kenneth Norris, thinks the sperm whale can aim a sound beam at squid. The beam would knock the squid out so that the whale could eat it with no trouble.

Sperm whales are a rare sight at sea. Even a glimpse of one, like this, is thrilling to an ocean-voyaging human.
KEN BALCOMB/ORES

Humpback Feeding

Humpbacks don't eat while they are in the tropics in the winter, caring for young babies and mating. So during the summer, they eat lots of food. They must store enough blubber to last them through the rest of the year. Each day, a feeding humpback needs about a ton of food containing about a million calories. That's enough to last an average human more than a year.

Humpbacks feed on small fish and little shrimplike animals that live in the sea. When there is lots of food, such as a big school of fish, the whale will come up to it from the side or underneath. Then it lunges through the water with its mouth open as it comes to the surface. The grooves on its underside expand, making its throat swell. Then the whale squeezes the water out through the baleen. The fringes of the baleen act like a sieve and keep the food in the whale's mouth.

These humpbacks are lunge feeding. The one in front is lying on its side. You can see the throat grooves and a flipper. The one behind has just come up with a mouthful. You can see the top of its head and water splashing out of its mouth. Notice the knobs on its head. KEN BALCOMB/ORES

Humpback bubble feeding. STEVEN MORELLO

    Humpbacks also use bubbles to help trap food. One way of bubble feeding is to circle underwater while blowing bubbles. The bubble circle keeps the food animals together. Then the whale comes up inside the circle with its mouth open.

    Humpbacks often feed in groups. They join in building bubble nets and in lunge feeding. In Alaska, the same whales have returned to one area for several years to feed together.

How other Baleen Whales Feed

Some baleen whales, like the blue and bowhead, swim along the surface of the water with their mouths open. The baleen strains out food as the whale swims. Blue whales also dive for food and take in huge amounts of water. They look like enormous tadpoles with their throats swollen with water and food. The water is squeezed out, leaving the food behind.

The fin whale circles around a school of fish. The fish seem to be startled by the white color on the right side of its face. This makes the fish huddle closer together. Then the whale opens its big mouth and lunges through the school.

The baleen of gray whales is coarse. They do not feed on the small animals other whales often eat. Instead, they skim food along the bottom of the sea. They sometimes take seaweed into their mouths and wash animals off it, too.

This fin whale is feeding on its side. You can see clearly the expanding throat grooves and the open mouth. ALISA SCHULMAN

6
Finding Out about the World

Like other mammals, whales have eyes, ears, and a nose. They can feel and touch and can taste their food. But their senses are quite different from ours.

The eye of a humpback whale is right by the corner of its mouth, where the curve of the lower jaw begins.
J. MICHAEL WILLIAMSON

The Eyes of Whales

Humans rely on sight more than on other senses. But in the water, eyes are not as useful as on land. An animal can't see as far underwater as on land. Light reaches only the upper layers of the water. At 600 feet (183 meters) deep, it is almost completely dark. We use vision to locate where we are. But out at sea, there are few landmarks to help an animal know its location. For all these reasons, whales do not rely very much on their eyes.

The whale's eyes are set back on the sides of the head. It can only see out to the side with each eye. It can't look straight in front. When a whale wants to see what is going on at the surface, it lifts its head straight out of the water. This is called "spy-hopping." Killer whales and gray whales are especially likely to spy-hop.

Whales can use their eyes out of water when they spy-hop, like this gray whale.
© BRUCE M. WELLMAN

Ears and Hearing

Some sounds carry for miles through the water, and sound moves about five times faster in water than in the air. So it is no surprise that sound is very important to whales.

Whales' ears are hard to see. On the outside, they show only as small holes behind the eyes. No one knows for sure just how whales hear. The inside parts of a whale's ear are surrounded by hollow spaces filled with foamy material. This helps protect the ears from pressure when the whale dives.

Some scientists think sound is carried to the ears through channels of fat or by the lower jawbones. But others believe that the foam-filled spaces keep such sounds from reaching the ears.

We may not know just how sound reaches the ears. But we do know that whales use sound to "see" their way around. This is called "echolocation" (ek-oh-lo-CAY-shun). If you stand on the

If you look closely, you can see both the eye and the ear of this killer whale in the shadow between the two white spots. LINDA CAMPBELL/THE WHALE MUSEUM

edge of a canyon and yell "Hello," you soon hear your voice come back to you. This is because sound bounces off solid objects. Whales make special sounds and then listen to hear them come back. This way, they can identify objects. They can tell how big something is and how far away it is.

Smell and Touch

Most mammals can smell quite well, but whales can't. Smell isn't very useful in water. Air carries the chemicals that we smell quickly. But they move more slowly in water. The nerves for smell are present in baleen whales, but not in toothed whales. Smell is really an important part of taste. So it seems strange that captive toothed whales sometimes have favorite foods.

Whales have a sense of touch. Touch is probably important in their social life, and some whales seem to enjoy being petted by people.

Touch is very important to some whales. Here, one whale is touching the other with its flipper during courtship. ALISA SCHULMAN

7
"Talking" to Each Other

Many whales are social animals. They live together and need ways of "talking" to each other, of communicating.

Humpback whales use different sounds to communicate. Here, a baby stays close to its mother while another whale swims nearby.
KEN BALCOMB / ORES

These belugas have bent their necks to look at each other.
KEN BALCOMB / ORES

Ways of Communicating

Unlike humans, most whales do not communicate by changing the expressions on their faces. But the beluga does. The beluga's neck bends, and its lips can change shape.

Belugas also communicate by clapping their jaws together. This makes a loud noise. Scientists think that sperm whales snap their jaws together to threaten each other. Male sperm whales probably also use their lower jaws to fight each other.

Jaws can be used to show caring, too. Adult sperm whales touch the young with their jaws. Sometimes they touch one another's jaws, as if kissing. Other kinds of touching can also be important to whales. Baby whales frequently stay right by their mothers so that the two whales are often touching.

Sounds with Messages

Whales use sound more than other ways of communicating. Fin whales make high-pitched sounds when they are near one another. Scientists think these sounds carry messages. The whales also make low-pitched sounds that can travel far through the water. These noises probably allow the whales to communicate over long distances.

Belugas are so noisy they are called "sea canaries." They make hundreds of different sounds, including trills, whistles, squeaks, and grunts. The variety of their sounds is amazing. They can sound like a screaming woman or a rusty hinge. They may whinny like a horse or cry like a baby.

Fin whales, like this mother and her calf, use different sorts of sounds to communicate with one another. STEVEN MORELLO

Humpback Songs

The most famous whale sounds are the songs of humpback whales. In many ways, these complex songs are like our human songs. They have themes that repeat, with beginnings and endings. They are sung the same way over and over again and last about a half-hour. Each whale in one area sings the same song, but with some small differences. From one year to the next, the song can change.

It appears that only male humpbacks sing. They do it during the breeding season, so scientists think the songs attract females or keep away other males. The songs can be heard at least 20 miles (30 kilometers) away.

Humpbacks are one of the most familiar whales to people. They may come very close to whale watching boats, as this one did in Massachusetts Bay.
J. MICHAEL WILLIAMSON

Breaching

Nothing shows the great strength of whales more than breaching. In breaching, the whale launches most or all of its body out of the water. Then it falls back again with a thundering splash. Humpback, right, gray, and sperm whales are most likely to breach. While many people have seen this awesome sight, no one knows for sure what it means to the whales. Because the sound is so loud and the splash so great, some scientists think breaching communicates a message of some sort to other whales. Whales breach during the breeding season, so it may be a part of courtship. But they also do it while feeding. For this reason, some scientists think it may also be used to stun or panic fish.

A young killer whale tests its strength by breaching.
© PETER THOMAS

44

8
Whales and People

This humpback was killed by Alaskan whalers in 1938. NOAA

Saving Whales

People have hunted whales for hundreds of years. Until the sixteenth century, only small numbers of whales were taken. But then whaling became big business. Whale oil was good for many purposes, such as fuel and making soap. In the days before plastic, baleen was handy for making things like shoehorns and fishing rods, because it is strong but flexible. Whale meat was good to eat.

In the 1860s, the exploding harpoon and motorized catcher boat were invented. These allowed whalers to chase down the fastest kinds of whales. Later on, huge factory ships allowed dead whales to be turned into oil on the open seas. Hundreds of thousands of whales were killed until some kinds were almost gone.

In 1946 the International Whaling Commission was set up. Many countries concerned about the future of whales joined. For years, the commission met to set limits on how many of each of the great whales—the biggest kinds—could be killed that year. But lots of people were worried that limiting hunting was not enough. There seemed to be too few whales already.

In 1983 the commission voted to stop almost all whaling beginning in 1985. Only a few whales could be taken by native peoples. But some countries have continued to kill whales. They say the end of whaling would be too hard on some of their people.

Chemical spills, like the one that killed this gray whale, are yet another enemy of whales and other sea life.
PAT MOORE / GREENPEACE

Whales as Friends

People feel close to whales, partly because whales have strong family ties. Like their relatives, the dolphins, whales sometimes show interest in people. Wild gray whales in Mexican waters have come up to boats and let people pet them. Killer whales in captivity perform beautifully with their human trainers. They are so reliable that children from the audience can feed the whales and get "kisses" in return.

There are many things we still don't know about whales. Perhaps the more we learn, the closer we will feel to these strange giants.

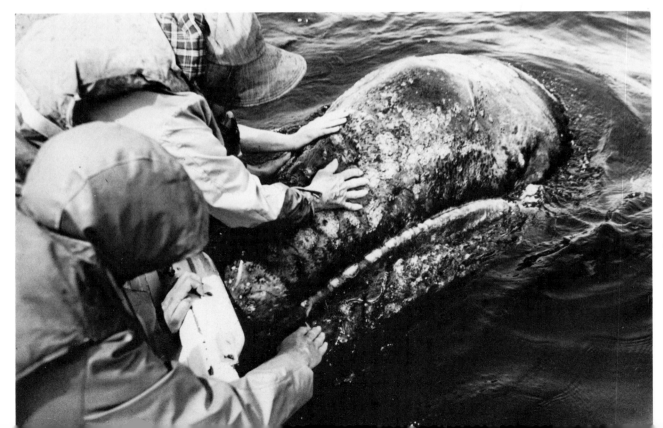

Whale watchers stroke a gray whale in San Ignacio Lagoon in Mexico.
© *BRUCE M. WELLMAN*

47

Index

(Italicized numbers indicate photos.)

3   7 5

J 599.51 P   51236
Patent, Dorothy Hinshaw.
All about whales $12.95

S-1/14 LV-10/11   44circs 6libs